GASTORNIS

PREHISTORIC BEASTS
GASTORNIS

MARC ZABLUDOFF
ILLUSTRATED BY PETER BOLLINGER

Marshall Cavendish
Benchmark
New York

Marshall Cavendish Benchmark
99 White Plains Road
Tarrytown, NY 10591
www.marshallcavendish.us

All Internet addresses were correct and accurate at the time of printing.

Library of Congress Cataloging-in-Publication Data

Zabludoff, Marc.
Gastornis / by Marc Zabludoff ; illustrated by Peter Bollinger.
p. cm.—(Prehistoric beasts)
Includes bibliographical references and index.
Summary: "Explore the flightless gastornis, its physical characteristics,
when and where it lived, how it lived, what other animals lived alongside
it, and how we know this"—Provided by publisher.
ISBN 978-0-7614-4000-0
1. Gastornis—Juvenile literature. 2. Birds, Fossil—Juvenile literature.
I. Title.
QE872.G27A33 2010
568—dc22
2008035939

Editor: Christine Florie
Publisher: Michelle Bisson
Art Director: Anahid Hamparian
Series Designer: Alicia Mikles

Photo research by Connie Gardner

The photographs in this book are used by permission and through the courtesy of:
Corbis: Tim Wright, 11; Peter Arnold Inc.: Biosphoto/Sylvestre Jean-Pierre, 17; American Museum of Natural History, 21.

Printed in Malaysia
1 3 5 6 4 2

CONTENTS

FEATHERED TERROR

High in the sky, the sun shines down on Earth with all its power. But in the middle of the thick forest, only thin, scattered rays of light make it through the leafy treetops and down to the forest floor. There a pair of small, speckled brown animals are happily nibbling at the tender leaves of a low-growing bush. In size and shape they look like small dogs, but their faces are more deerlike. Millions of years from now their **descendants** will in fact be deer, and their bodies will have grown. Here, though, these deer ancestors look like leaf-eating puppies.

Above them, crawling easily along a thick branch, a furry, long-clawed, black-and-white insect-eater busily searches the bark for food. Higher still, a loud assembly of birds flits through the treetops, filling the hot, moist air with honks and shrill whistles.

Another bird is also on the scene. But this one is quiet. It stands upright,

Hidden deep within the lush forest, *Gastornis* stalks its prey.

and not on a tree but next to it, on the ground. This bird is huge, at least 6 feet tall, and much bigger than any other animal around. Despite its size, it keeps so still that the tiny deer, just 30 feet away, might easily mistake its thick legs for slender tree trunks. But the deer do not even notice it. Walking delicately on their toes, they move ever nearer to the giant bird as they search among the leaves for ripe berries.

If the insect-eater in the tree above them had not suddenly dashed noisily up the tree trunk, the little deer might never have noticed the giant bird in time. Without pausing to think, they whirl away from the bushes and start running wildly through leaves, around trees, over roots, and under hanging vines, twisting and turning as fast as they can. Right behind them the feathered beast runs, its huge feet thundering on the ground. Nearly on top of the panicked deer, the bird opens its enormous beak and slices downward.

But this time the beak comes up empty. The deer have escaped. The great bird gives up its chase, stands still, and patiently waits for another meal to come wandering by.

In an instant, *Gastornis* lunges through the brush for its meal. ➡

DEADLY FROM NOSE TO TOES

The feathered terror of the forest was named *Gastornis*, and it first appeared on Earth about 56 million years ago. It stood 6 to 7 feet tall, its body balanced atop two thick legs. At the bottom of those legs were large, menacing feet, each sprouting three long, forward-pointing toes tipped with sharp, deadly claws.

Gastornis had a body that was broad, muscular, and very heavy. Unlike most birds, which need to be lightweight so they can fly, *Gastornis* had no need to get off the ground. Its ancestors had given up flying long before. They found they could live and eat better by staying on the ground. So they grew bigger, stronger, and heavier. *Gastornis* weighed at least 200 pounds and perhaps as much as 400 pounds.

Gastornis went **extinct** around 41 million years ago, and all we have left of it are its bones. So we cannot be absolutely sure what it looked like. But since it was a bird, it was certainly covered with feathers. Its

Gastornis and the American robin are both birds. How many differences between them can you find?

NAME BLAME

It would be nice if *Gastornis* meant something like "really big, scary beast with an awesome beak," but unfortunately, all it means is "Gaston's bird." It was named in 1855 after Gaston Planté, the French scientist who first found the bird's **fossil** bones.

long legs were probably bare. Its face might have been bare of feathers also, like the face of a vulture.

Like most birds, its body was more or less football-shaped. At one end was a short tail. At the other end was an enormously powerful, thick neck and a large, 1.5-foot-long head. Forming the front of this horse-size head was the bird's most fearsome weapon: a huge, hatchet-shaped beak,

11

Gastornis's most prominent feature was its fierce beak.

strong enough to crush the bones of any animal unlucky enough to be caught in its bite.

The only unimpressive parts of Gastornis were its wings. They were tiny stumps, so small that it is hard to imagine what Gastornis did with them. They looked as out of place on this giant bird as the tiny front legs do on a Tyrannosaurus rex. Of course, tiny limbs were not the only thing the giant bird and the giant dinosaur had in common.

DINO IN DISGUISE?

Gastornis was unlike any bird found on Earth today. But then, its world was unlike the world we live in today.

Fifty-six million years ago, there were few other really big animals to be found anywhere on Earth. By then all the dinosaurs had been gone for 9 million years. The mammals scurrying over the land were mostly small plant-eaters and insect-eaters. Even the **carnivores**—the meat-eaters—were no bigger than dogs. Most were the size of weasels or foxes.

It was a time when any large, meat-eating creatures could have the world at their command. Today these animals are almost always mammals, such as lions, polar bears, and humans. But after the dinosaurs died off, the animals that first grabbed this opportunity were birds.

13

WAS *GASTORNIS* THE BIGGEST BIRD THAT EVER LIVED?

Actually, no. Several later birds, all now extinct, were bigger. New Zealand's moas grew as tall as 11 or 12 feet and weighed more than 500 pounds. The elephant birds of Madagascar grew to be only (!)10 feet tall but weighed a whopping 1,000 pounds. Neither moas nor elephant birds were meat-eaters. But the terror birds of South America were. They were lighter than *Gastornis*, but some were taller—up to 9 feet—and they were fast runners, too.

Elephant Bird   **Moa**   **Terror Bird**   **Gastornis**

A world ruled by giant, flightless birds might seem odd to us. Yet it makes sense. Most scientists now agree that birds are actually descendants of the dinosaurs. That is, over many millions of years, one type of dinosaur gradually **evolved**, or changed, into the creatures we know as birds. Their jaws became beaks, their scales became feathers, and their arms became wings.

Certainly, gazing at *Gastornis*'s skeleton, the idea is easy to understand. Put some teeth in its beak, and it begins to look like a small *T. rex*, ready to grab and devour any animal that crosses its path.

BIRD LAND

Gastornis lived across a wide area. There is some confusion about just how wide, though. The first *Gastornis* bones were found in France in 1855. About twenty years later the bones of another giant bird were found in North America, in the desert of New Mexico. At the time the discoverers did not recognize how similar the two fossil birds were. The North American bird—which, at 7 feet, was about a foot taller than the French bird—was given a different name, *Diatryma*, by the **paleontologist** Edward Drinker Cope.

Since then, *Gastornis* fossils have been found throughout Europe, and *Diatryma* fossils have been found in many spots in North America—from New Mexico and Colorado to New Jersey. Today, a number of scientists think *Gastornis* and *Diatryma* were so similar that they should both be called by the same name. At the very least the two birds were closely related.

Though *Diatryma* did not live in the same region as *Gastornis*, some scientists think that the birds were closely related.

The places they lived in were very similar, too. Nobody would confuse New Mexico and France today, but 56 million years ago, Earth was rather

different. The planet was much warmer than it is now. There was no ice at the North and South Poles. Much of Earth's land was covered with dense, moist forests, like the rain forests found only in the **tropics** today.

Those forests were a perfect home for *Gastornis*. Surrounded by trees, vines, and leaves, even a giant like *Gastornis* could hide if it wanted.

It probably did want to hide, too. Not out of fear—there was no animal, except perhaps another of its own kind, that could threaten it. *Gastornis* hid because it needed to catch its **prey** by surprise. *Gastornis* was so big and heavy that it could not have been a very good runner. Besides, the thick forests were not easy to run in. But with its

WORLD TRAVELERS

If *Gastornis*, in Europe, and *Diatryma*, in North America, were closely related, then some of their ancestors must have traveled from one **continent** to the other. But neither bird could fly or swim across an ocean, so how did they do it? They walked. At that time, northern Europe and North America were connected by land, and there was no ice in the Arctic to stop a wandering bird in its tracks.

← **Millions of years ago, *Gastornis* lived in tropical regions, sharing its home with a variety of animals.**

long legs, fearsome feet, and beastly beak, *Gastornis* could easily grab any animal it got close enough to.

The forests were filled with tasty items for a big hungry bird—among them the ancestors of deer and horses. Those ancient animals were much smaller than they are now. Early horses, for example, were no bigger than a golden retriever, and most were closer to the size of a fox. They fed on leaves and fruit rather than on grass, and they scurried about on feet that still had separate toes rather than a single hoof.

SILENT BONES

Nearly everything we know about *Gastornis* comes from the fossil bones it left behind. This evidence tells us a lot, but it cannot tell us everything. For example, we know how big and strong *Gastornis* was from its skeleton, and we know what its beak and claws looked like. One glance at that foot-long, heavy beak is enough to convince most people that *Gastornis* was a hunter to be feared. But we actually do not know that for certain.

Some scientists argue that the big bird's beak does not really resemble the beak of any other meat-eating bird we know of—it

This *Gastornis* fossil is evidence that such a bird existed and provides scientists with some clues about its life.

21

does not have a hook at the end, as does the beak of a hawk. They say it is possible that *Gastornis* actually used its beak not for crushing bones but for cracking open nuts, like a parrot does.

Still, it is hard to see why any nut-cracking bird would need a beak a foot long, even for the biggest nuts. So most scientists think *Gastornis* was indeed a meat-eater. More probably, though, it was both a hunter and a **scavenger**—that is, it ambushed live animals and also eagerly ate any already-dead animals it came across. Many modern meat-eating birds, such as eagles, are part-time scavengers as well.

Likewise, we can only make our best guess as to what *Gastornis*'s family life was like. In its warm, forested world *Gastornis* was easily the biggest kid on the block. Once it was fully grown, it had nothing to fear from any other **predator**. But eggs and newly hatched chicks needed protection. Those fast-growing chicks

DO WE KNOW WHAT COLOR GASTORNIS WAS?

Not really. But to catch its prey by surprise, *Gastornis* needed to blend in with the forest. So its legs and lower body were probably dull brown or black. Its upper body, though, and especially its huge beak, might have been as bright as any tropical bird's and colored yellow, red, blue, or green.

had to be fed, too, until they were big enough to hunt for themselves.

So *Gastornis* probably laid only one or two eggs at a time. Even the busiest meat-eating giant bird would find it hard to feed and protect more chicks than that.

Scientists think that *Gastornis*'s young were protected by their mothers until they could fend for themselves.

THE END OF A GIANT

Gastornis could not rule as king of the forest forever. After 15 million years *Gastornis* disappeared, and its role as top predator was taken over by furry, sharp-toothed mammals.

Why did these powerful birds die out? It is hard to come up with a complete answer to that question. It was not because there was anything wrong with *Gastornis*. It was an animal well suited for its world. However, the world is always changing, and animals are not always able to change with it.

By 41 million years ago Earth had grown cooler and drier than it had been when *Gastornis* first appeared. The planet was not cold—there was yet no ice at the North Pole—and *Gastornis* certainly could have kept warm enough. But the change in **climate** caused a change in the kinds of trees that grew in the big bird's home in North America and Europe. The

As Earth cooled, *Gastornis*'s world changed, ➡ threatening its existence forever.

forests became more like the northern woods we know today and less like the rain forests of the tropics.

Instead of growing all year round, leaves and fruits appeared only in the spring and summer. Animals that needed to eat those leaves and fruits all the time—animals that *Gastornis* depended on for food—disappeared.

At the same time, many new types of mammals evolved. Among them were some that may have been better at stealing and eating *Gastornis*'s large eggs. They also might have been better at burrowing under the forest floor, out of the big bird's sight. Larger, faster carnivores appeared also, and they may have made it harder for *Gastornis* to find enough food.

In the end, these changes were too much for the huge birds, and slowly they began to vanish. Their deadly claws no longer tore at the forest floor; their killing beaks no longer sliced through the air. Today, the feathered giants live on only in our books and museums.

TIMELINE

380–375 million years ago	First four-legged animals appear.
340–310 million years ago	First reptiles appear.
230–225 million years ago	First dinosaurs and mammals appear.
160–150 million years ago	First birds appear.
65 million years ago	Dinosaurs become extinct.
63 million years ago	Earth becomes warmer and wetter.
56 million years ago	Ancestors of hoofed mammals, such as deer and horses, appear; first ancestors of true primates (lemurs, monkeys, apes, and humans) appear; first bats appear; *Gastornis* and *Diatryma* appear.
50 million years ago	Global temperatures peak; afterward Earth begins to turn cooler and drier; gradually, plants become more seasonal in the north.
41 million years ago	*Gastornis* and *Diatryma* become extinct.

GLOSSARY

carnivore	animal that eats meat.
climate	average kind of weather in a particular place over a long time period.
continent	any one of the seven great bodies of land on Earth.
descendants	all of an animal's offspring through the generations.
evolve	to change over time.
extinct	gone forever.
fossil	remains of an animal or plant that lived long ago.
paleontologist	person who studies forms of life from prehistoric times.
predator	animal that hunts and eats other animals.
prey	animal that is hunted and eaten by a predator.
scavenger	meat-eater that eats dead animals not killed by itself.
tropics	areas around the middle of the planet where it is nearly always hot.

FIND OUT MORE

Books

Lappi, Megan. *Birds* (Prehistoric Life). New York: Weigl Publishers, 2004.

Linden, Carol K. *Terror Bird* (Extinct Monsters). Mankato, MN: Capstone Press, 2007.

DVD

Walking with Prehistoric Beasts. (DVD) BBC/Warner Home Video, 2002.

Web Site

Walking with Prehistoric Beasts

http://dsc.discovery.com/convergence/beasts/beasts.html

At this Discovery Channel site, visit a prehistoric zoo, look at images in its beast gallery, and take a beastly quiz.

INDEX

Page numbers in **boldface** are illustrations.

ABOUT THE AUTHOR

Marc Zabludoff, the former editor in chief of *Discover* magazine, has been involved in communicating science to the public for more than two decades. His other work for Marshall Cavendish includes books on spiders, beetles, and monkeys in the AnimalWays series, along with books on insects, reptiles, and the largely unknown and chiefly microscopic organisms known as protoctists. Zabludoff lives in New York City with his wife and daughter.

ABOUT THE ILLUSTRATOR

Peter Bollinger is an award-winning illustrator whose clients include those in the publishing, advertising, and entertainment industries. Bollinger works in two separate styles, traditional airbrush and digital illustration. He lives in California with his wife, son, and daughter.